MOMMY MAGIC

A Transformational Guide for Spiritual Mompreneurs

*How to Master Mindset & Manifestation
to Increase Income & Impact*

ANDREA KAYE

© 2025 ALL RIGHTS RESERVED.

Published by She Rises Studios Publishing **www.SheRisesStudios.com.**

No part of this book may be reproduced or transmitted in any form whatsoever, electronic, or mechanical, including photocopying, recording, or by any informational storage or retrieval system without the expressed written, dated and signed permission from the publisher and author.

LIMITS OF LIABILITY/DISCLAIMER OF WARRANTY:

The author and publisher of this book have used their best efforts in preparing this material. While every attempt has been made to verify the information provided in this book, neither the author nor the publisher assumes any responsibility for any errors, omissions, or inaccuracies.

The author and publisher make no representation or warranties with respect to the accuracy, applicability, or completeness of the contents of this book. They disclaim any warranties (expressed or implied), merchantability, or for any purpose. The author and publisher shall in no event be held liable for any loss or other damages, including but not limited to special, incidental, consequential, or other damages.

ISBN: 978-1-969463-92-1

Introduction

This book is dedicated to my WHY my children, my WORLD. Amadeus, Leilani, Valencia and Zyan aka "Chunk", I do it all for you. Follow Your Dreams. Live with passion, power and purpose. You were made for greatness. I'm so very grateful to be your mommy. I love you my babies with all of my heart. Heart means love and love is the answer.

You've always known you were meant for more - more impact, more freedom, more alignment.

You've healed, grown, and awakened to who you truly are. But now, a quiet voice inside whispers, *"It's time to lead."*

Still, doubt creeps in.

Who am I to start a business? Can I really turn my calling into income?

Between motherhood and responsibilities, it's easy to shrink your dreams to fit your comfort zone.

Mommy Magic is your energetic reset - a guide to recoding your subconscious, releasing the old "good girl" and "supermom" patterns, and stepping into the magnetic creator you were born to be.

In these pages, you'll learn how to:

- Reprogram your beliefs around money, visibility, and self-worth
- Align your energy with the business and life you truly desire
- Tap into the Magnetic Mind method to manifest success from flow, not force
- Balance soulful motherhood with authentic entrepreneurship

You're not here to hustle harder - you're here to *vibrate higher*.

Make SHIFT Happen. Let's GROW.

Table of Contents

CHAPTER 1

My Message – Chaos to Conscious Creation – Activating My Mommy Magic

There was a time when I felt like I was doing everything "right"- but nothing felt right inside.

Motherhood. Relationships. Money. I was showing up, grinding, giving... but deep down, I was disconnected. I looked successful on the outside but felt stuck on the inside. Sound familiar?

That's when everything shifted.

That's when I remembered who I was.

I AM that I AM. I am not my past I am who I choose to become. I am Andrea the Magnetic Mompreneur.

I'm a 40-year-old, homebirthing, unschooling mompreneur of 4 from Pennsylvania, and I'm obsessed (like can't-sleep-when-the-downloads-hit obsessed) with human transformation and the process of creation. I'm also an international and Amazon bestselling author of a collaborative book- Dream Big Do Bigger- Build the Bridge Between Your Dreams & Reality- with my chapter "Holy SHIFT. I AM the Bridge" and my first solo book Dumbed Down Drugged Up & Disempowered Awakening and Making the Shift into the Quantum New 5D Earth Paradigm: A Transformational Guide to Liberate Humanity.

I am a superconscious creator and transformation accelerator. I help you awaken to your divine soul TRUTH, find your purpose and take your power back.

I didn't just write a book. I wrote a wake-up call.

Dumbed Down, Drugged Up & Disempowered is for anyone who feels the pull. Those who know there's more. The spiritual seekers, ready to unplug from the programming and reclaim their sovereignty.

We are in the middle of a mass awakening- a SHIFT in consciousness. And YOU are part of the EVOLution rEVOLution.

We are not here to hustle ourselves into exhaustion.

We are here to align, activate, and ascend.

You can get your FREE PDF Copy of the book @ **www.QuantumMemberSHIFT.space/AndreaKaye**

Waking Up to What I Truly Desired

The Magnetic Mind process taught me something radical: my desires were not wrong, selfish, or impossible. They were sacred.

For the first time, I gave myself permission to want what I *actually* wanted and not what society told me I should want. I wanted time freedom. Soulful impact. Overflowing abundance. A passionate, loving relationship. A thriving business. And I wanted to raise my children in joy, not burnout.

This was the first key to becoming magnetic: **alignment with true desires.** Not survival. Not hustle. But desire.

Reprogramming the Inner Voice That Said "You Can't"

Let's be real- every mompreneur carries limiting beliefs like emotional baggage in her diaper bag.

"I'm not enough."
"I'm too late."
"I'm selfish to want more."

The Rapid Recode process helped me identify and dissolve those subconscious blocks, gently but powerfully. I began to rewire my brain and body for success, joy, and ease. I was no longer trapped by my past. I was rewriting my story as I lived it.

And that story? It was magic.

Creating From the Future, Not the Past

The Magnetic Mind approach isn't just about mindset- it's about **structure**. Clear, deliberate, energetic structure.

Every day, I began visualizing and *feeling* my dream life as if it were already done. I embodied her- *the successful, radiant, magnetic version of me.* The more I lived in that energy, the faster my reality caught up.

This wasn't just manifestation fluff. This was deep, integrated, transformational work.

Why This Matters for YOU, Mama

If you're reading this, chances are you feel the same pull I once felt.

You're tired of playing small. You crave more, even if you can't fully admit it yet. You know there's magic in you, but you're not sure how to unlock it between laundry piles and launch plans.

That's where my mission was born.

Today, I guide other spiritual mompreneurs through this same Magnetic Mind process- because it *works*. It's not a surface-level pep talk. It's a reactivation of your *true creator self.* It's your shortcut through the chaos, straight into your core power.

How I Rewired My Mind and Recoded My Life

When I discovered the Magnetic Mind method, I finally had language for what my soul already knew: I am the creator of my reality. And the Rapid Recode process gave me the tools to become that creator on every level- mentally, emotionally, spiritually, on a deep cellular level.

I've trained as a certified Magnetic Mind Coach, NLP Practitioner, EFT & Time Techniques specialist, Hypnotherapist, Life & Success Coach, Intuitive Healing, Akashic Records Practitioner, Human Design and a Master Certification in the Alchemy of Integrative coaching. I combine ancient spiritual truths of alchemy and universal law with neuroscience, epigenetics, and quantum physics to help spiritual mompreneurs like you, *recode your DNA* and *manifest your dream life.*

Yes, it's real.
Yes, it works.
Yes, you can do it too.

The Mission: From Mom Mode to Magnetism

Since 2020, I've been helping women like you remember your divine truth, ditch the toxic conditioning, and step into the most powerful version of themselves.

A Life of Alignment, Abundance, and Authenticity

Now, I don't just run a business- I run a movement.

I teach other women to master their emotions, align with their soul's calling, take action from clarity, and become unstoppable. We do the inner work together so we can create real outer success- with spaciousness, softness, and unapologetic ambition.

That's the mommy magic.

That's the new paradigm of leadership.

And that's what's waiting for you.

This Is Just the Beginning.

You're not crazy. You're not broken. You're not lazy.

You're waking up. You're rising. You're remembering.

If you're on a holistic health, spiritual awakening, or personal growth journey, YOU ARE IN THE RIGHT PLACE.

You're not meant to fit in. You're meant to lead.

Let's raise the frequency of this planet together. One mama. One miracle. One mindset shift at a time.

Truth, Love & Light,

Namaste

Andrea Kaye

The Magnetic Mompreneur 🧲

🐟 Mommy Magic Activation Exercise: Recode, Remember, Rise

This isn't just a chapter- it's a wake-up call. Now let's move from inspiration into integration.

Take a few quiet minutes, light a candle if it feels good, and tune in. Let your truth rise.

✍️ Journal Prompts:

Where am I living by "shoulds" instead of soul desires?

(Example: "I should be grateful." vs "I desire time freedom and creative expression.")

____

____

____

____

____

What do I truly want without shame, guilt, or fear of being "too much"?

(List 3 big desires, no editing, no shrinking.)

1. ____

2. ____

3. ____

What limiting belief is keeping me stuck?

(Example: "I can't make money doing what I love.")

____

____

____

Who do I get to become to create the life I desire?

(Visualize and describe the magnetic, fully expressed YOU.)

____

____

____

What is one aligned action I will take this week to move toward that vision?

(Small steps count. Inspired action compounds and creates momentum.)

____

____

____

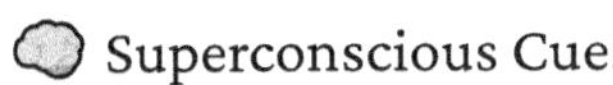 Superconscious Cue:

"I choose to remember who I am. I am a powerful creator. I am safe to want what I want. And I choose it now."

Say it. Feel it. Own it.

Bonus Alignment Ritual:

Magnetic Mirror Time

Each morning, look into your own eyes in the mirror and say:

"I am worthy. My desires are divine. I create with ease, grace, and joy."

This activates your subconscious and anchors the new identity.

You are no longer just surviving motherhood. You are magnetizing miracles.

You're not stuck- you're shifting.

Keep going, Mama. You are the rEVOLution.

Make SHIFT Happen. Let's GROW.

CHAPTER 2

Motherhood – We Are Powerful Creators

Motherhood is one of the most profound initiations a woman can experience. It is not just the act of nurturing a child, it is a spiritual awakening, a mirror that reflects both our greatest strengths and our hidden limitations. In many ways, becoming a mother is a rebirth of the self.

When a child enters your life, you are called to grow beyond who you were. The sleepless nights, the constant demands, and the moments of sheer overwhelm are not just challenges, they are opportunities for transformation. Motherhood invites us to peel away layers of old identity and reconnect with our truest essence.

Activation: Reclaiming Wholeness

Close your eyes, place your hand on your heart, and whisper: "I am enough as I am. My children need my wholeness, not my perfection." Breathe this in until it feels like truth.

Motherhood is a sacred journey, but it can also feel overwhelming when the days blur together in endless to-do lists and responsibilities. That's why a powerful morning practice can shift everything. The SAVERS method-Silence, Affirmations, Visualization, Exercise, Reading, and Scribing-offers a simple yet life-changing framework for creating mornings that nurture both your soul and your business dreams. When you combine this with a Magnetic Mind morning routine, you're not just ticking off tasks, you're aligning with your true desires, reprogramming limiting beliefs, and stepping into the creative structure of the woman you're meant to be. Add in the wisdom of the 80/20 principle- focusing your energy on the 20% of actions that create 80% of results, strong, powerful, aligned, purposeful action and suddenly your days feel lighter, more intentional, and filled with flow. Science also backs this up: transcendental meditation, for example, has been proven to reduce stress, boost clarity, and increase creativity, exactly what every mompreneur needs to stay grounded and magnetic. When you start your day in this empowered state, you show up for your family, your business, and yourself in a way that feels aligned, abundant, and deeply fulfilling. Learn more about Transcendental Meditation at **TM.org**

Motherhood also isn't about creating a perfect schedule, it's about creating a rhythm that nourishes both you and your little ones. Conscious parenting, homebirth, and unschooling all come from the same heart-centered place: trusting your intuition and honoring your family's natural flow. Instead of rigid routines, think in terms of rituals- morning cuddles that set the tone for the day, shared meals that anchor your family in connection, and quiet moments for rest and reflection. These gentle structures give children the safety they need to grow, while giving you the space to breathe, heal, and align with your deeper desires. When you allow your daily rhythm to be guided by love and presence rather than pressure, you create a home environment that naturally promotes healing, creativity, and growth- for both you and your children.

 Sample Daily Flow for a Healing + Growth-Oriented Home

Morning Grounding (7–9 AM)

Wake slowly, cuddle in bed, gratitude or affirmations with the kids.

Gentle breakfast together- invite your children to help with simple tasks (pouring, stirring, setting the table).

Light movement: stretching, yoga, or a short nature walk.

Exploration & Play (9–12 PM)

Follow curiosity: reading stories, playing outside, art projects, baking, gardening.

Keep invitations open-ended rather than structured lessons.

Use natural moments for learning (measuring ingredients, observing bugs, asking questions).

Midday Reset (12–2 PM)

Shared lunch- encourage conversation about feelings, ideas, or what excites them.

Quiet time: naps, journaling, drawing, or independent play while you recharge.

Creative Flow (2–5 PM)

Music, building forts, crafts, kitchen experiments, or a family project.

Trips to the park, library, or museum if you feel like venturing out.

Encourage kids to take the lead in choosing activities.

Evening Connection (5–8 PM)

Cook dinner together- let kids chop veggies, stir sauces, or set the table.

Family dinner ritual: candles, gratitude, storytelling.

Gentle wind-down: baths, reading aloud, singing, or sharing "best parts of the day."

Nighttime Nourishment (8–10 PM)

Cozy bedtime routine: snuggles, prayers/intentions, soft music, read a book.

After kids are down, mama time: journaling, meditation, tea, or partner connection.

✨ The key: Hold the anchors (meals, rest, connection times) while leaving space for freedom, curiosity, and flow. This creates structure without rigidity, giving children safety and creativity, while giving you balance and peace.

The Spiritual Mirror of Motherhood

Every tantrum, every milestone, every tiny hand reaching for yours becomes a mirror. It reveals your patience, your triggers, your capacity for unconditional love, and your ability to surrender.

Many mothers find themselves wrestling with beliefs such as:

"I'm not doing enough."

"I have to sacrifice everything for my children."

"I can't have success and be a good mom at the same time."

These beliefs often come from childhood programming, cultural expectations, or inherited family narratives. They can quietly shape the way you show up as both a mother and a woman.

💭 ***Reflection Prompt: What beliefs about motherhood have I carried that no longer serve me?***

But here lies the truth: your children don't need a perfect mother. They need a whole mother. And wholeness comes when you allow yourself to release those limiting beliefs and step into alignment with your deepest desires.

The Magnetic Power of Motherhood

Motherhood is not a limitation, it is an amplifier. It expands your ability to love, to create, and to lead. When you align with your true desires, you model for your children what it means to live authentically and you can teach and lead by example.

Imagine the power of raising children who grow up watching their mother unapologetically follow her dreams, build a business she loves, and still be fully present in their lives. That is the magic of the spiritual mompreneur.

✨ Activation: Aligning with Desire

Visualize your life as both a mother and a woman fully lit up, your business thriving, your children joyful, your spirit expansive. Anchor it by declaring: "I choose alignment. I choose joy. I choose to model freedom for my children."

Reflection Prompt: How do I want my children to remember me, not just as their mother, but as a woman?

My Journey of Motherhood

My own path through motherhood has been nothing short of a spiritual initiation. I began with a C-section but I knew deep down that my story wasn't meant to end there. With courage and trust in my body's wisdom, I went on to experience a powerful VBAC, (vaginal birth after cesarean) allowing me to reclaim my inner strength. That awakening led me to embrace two unassisted homebirths- sacred, raw, and deeply empowering experiences that redefined how I see myself as both a mother and a creator. Now, as a homeschooling mompreneur raising four free-spirited children through the lens of unschooling, I embody the truth that motherhood and entrepreneurship are not opposing forces. They are both expressions of creation, freedom, and alignment with the life I choose to live.

Reflection Prompt: If I trusted that my desires make me a better mom, what would I allow myself to create?

The Balance Myth

One of the greatest lies sold to mothers is the idea of "balance." Balance suggests perfection, that you can give 100% to your business, 100% to your family, and still have 100% left for yourself. But the truth is, balance is fluid. Some days your business will need more of you. Some days your children will. And some days, you must fiercely choose yourself. That's real balance.

Instead of balance, think alignment. When you are aligned with your true desires and living in emotional mastery, the flow of life feels natural. You stop battling against guilt and start embracing grace.

✤ Activation: Embodying the Creator

Stand tall, feet grounded, arms open wide. Say aloud: "I am the creator of my reality. Just as I birthed my children, I birth my desires into the world."

💬 *Reflection Prompt: What legacy am I consciously choosing to build through both motherhood and entrepreneurship?*

The Transformational Invitation

Motherhood is not meant to break you down, it is meant to break you open. It is the initiation into a higher version of yourself, one that is capable of creating life both within the home and in the world. Remember just how powerful you are- you create life. You are the bridge between the spiritual and physical realms.

So, dear mama, release the pressure of perfection. Claim your desires boldly. Trust that your children are not holding you back- they are witnessing your transformation and will rise with you.

Motherhood is not the end of who you are. It is the portal to becoming everything you were always meant to be.

Make SHIFT Happen. Let's GROW.

CHAPTER 3

Manifestation Magic – Aligning with Your True Desires

*"The world is full of magic things,
patiently waiting for our senses to grow sharper."*
—William Butler Yeats

You already know there's more to life than just surviving nap time, (wait what's nap time?) juggling laundry, and building your business during stolen moments. Deep down, there's a fire inside you, a knowing that you're meant to create something meaningful, abundant, and joyful. That's the magic of manifestation. And mama, it's time you claimed it.

What Is Manifestation, Really?

Let's break the fluff: manifestation isn't just about "thinking positive" or making wish lists during a full moon. Manifestation is about becoming the version of you who already has what she desires. It's aligning your thoughts, emotions, and energy with that version of yourself, then letting the universe rearrange itself to meet you there.

And for spiritual mompreneurs, this isn't optional. It's essential.

Why? Because you're not just creating a business. You're creating a lifestyle. A legacy. A freedom-based life where you get to be present with your kids and build wealth doing what lights your soul on fire.

Step One: Claim What You Truly Want (Not What You've Settled For)

Most moms unknowingly manifest from guilt or obligation. "I just want enough to get by." "I don't need much, just enough to help my family."

No more crumbs.

The Magnetic Mind method teaches us to align with our true desires. Not the ones filtered through fear, society, or self-sacrifice. We start by asking, "What would I love?" not, "What's realistic?"

You are allowed to want more- more time, money, joy, impact- simply because you want it. That desire is your soul giving you direction. We are taught that wanting is wrong. We often ask the question, "Do I really need this or that?" In a world that primarily focuses on needs, this automatically puts us in a lack mindset in survival and we feel wanting things makes us a bad, greedy or ungrateful person.

Step Two: Clear the Inner Static

Manifestation fails when your subconscious programming is working against you. You can visualize abundance all day, but if your inner narrative says:

"I'm not good enough."

"Moms can't have it all."

"If I succeed, I'll lose time with my kids..."

...you'll unconsciously sabotage yourself.

That's where the Rapid Recode process from the Magnetic Mind method becomes life-changing. It helps you identify and recode those deep-seated beliefs into ones that support your vision. This isn't just mindset work. It's identity work- deep soul work. Because success isn't something you achieve, it's someone you become.

Success isn't personal- it's structural and we just have to reorient into a creative structure into flow.

Step Three: Feel It Now

The universe responds to frequency, not fantasy or delusion.

You can't wait until you hit your income goal to feel abundant. You have to feel abundant now. When you embody the emotional state of your desired outcome- joy, peace, gratitude- you magnetize experiences that match.

So here's your new mantra: "I don't chase, I attract. What belongs to me simply flows."

Step Four: Align with Inspired Action

Manifestation isn't passive. It's not about sitting on a yoga mat chanting affirmations while your business builds itself. Divine, aligned, inspired, INTENTIONAL action is required because faith without work is DEAD.

Once you're aligned, action becomes natural- joyful, even. You feel pulled rather than pushed. You know when to rest, when to post, when to launch. You stop overthinking and start trusting.

And you do it your way, not how some 7-figure marketer told you to.

Step Five: Be Her Now

The most powerful manifestation hack? Be her now.

Want to be a 6-figure mompreneur with balance and bliss? Start asking:

How does she handle challenges?

What does she believe about herself?

How does she speak, walk, parent, sell?

Act like her- not from a place of faking, but from remembering who you really are beneath the fear, fatigue, worry and doubt.

Manifestation Isn't Woo Woo- It's a Skill

When you understand how to work with your mind, your emotions, and your energy, manifestation becomes predictable.

No more hoping.
No more hustling.
Just clear, aligned, intentional creation.

Mama, the life you want already exists in a version of reality. Your only job is to align with it.

You're not too late.
You're not too tired.
You're not too anything.

You are powerful, magical, and you were born for this. You are meant to break the generational patterns, cycles and habits and create a legacy for generations to come. And the time is NOW.

❀ Reflection Questions

Desire vs. Settling ~ Am I currently creating from my true desires or from fear, guilt, or "just enough to get by"?

____

____

____

Identity Check ~ Who am I being right now, and is that version of me aligned with my vision?

____

____

____

Belief Audit ~ What are the top 3 beliefs that might be quietly sabotaging my dreams?

1. ____

2. ____

3. ____

Emotional Alignment ~ How often do I let myself feel the way I imagine I'll feel when my goal is achieved?

____

____

____

Action Alignment ~ Do my daily actions reflect faith in my vision or fear of failure?

____

____

____

✍️ Journal Prompts

If nothing and no one could judge me, here's what I would love to create in my business and life:

____

____

Write without editing ~ let your desires pour out uncensored.

My inner static sounds like...

List the doubts, fears, and old stories you hear in your mind. Then rewrite each one into a belief that supports your vision.

I am her now because...

Describe, in present tense, your day as the highest version of you. Where are you? Who are you with? How do you spend your time?

____

____

____

My next inspired action is...

____

____

____

Write down one aligned step you can take this week that feels exciting and expansive- not forced.

____

____

____

The legacy I'm creating:

Describe how your business and life choices will impact your children, community, and future generations.

____

____

____

🐦 Closing Mantra 🐦

"I am done with crumbs. I claim the feast. I am her now- abundant, powerful, magnetic. I create with joy, I act with faith, and I leave a legacy of freedom and love. The universe moves for me, and I receive it all with open arms."

Make SHIFT Happen. Let's GROW.

CHAPTER 4

Miracles – Magic & Miracles Are Both One & the Same

There's something magical about motherhood that science can't quite measure. Sure, we can explain hormones, biology, and sleepless nights with charts and studies- but there's a deeper truth we all feel in our bones: miracles are woven into the fabric of being a mom.

A miracle isn't always the dramatic, part-the-seas kind of event. Sometimes it's subtle. Sometimes it whispers. Sometimes it hides in plain sight, waiting for us to notice.

The first time you felt your baby kick inside you- that was a miracle.

The way your little one instinctively knew your heartbeat and calmed in your arms- that was a miracle.

Even now, in the messy moments- spilled juice, endless laundry, meltdowns in the grocery store- there's a miracle unfolding: you are shaping a human life with love.

Everyday Miracles

Miracles don't only show up in the big milestones like first steps or first words. They sneak into the tiniest corners of your day:

When your child suddenly says something so wise you wonder if an angel whispered it to them.

When you wake up exhausted but still find strength you didn't know you had.

When laughter bursts out of nowhere, breaking tension like sunlight through storm clouds.

These are not "small things." They're proof that you're supported, guided, and more powerful than you realize.

Miracles Begin in the Mind

Here's the secret most moms forget: miracles start on the inside.

When you shift your focus from what's going wrong to what's possible, you open the door to new outcomes. That shift isn't just "positive thinking"- it's you stepping into your creative power.

According to the Magnetic Mind Method, miracles aren't random accidents. They happen when your desires, beliefs, and emotions line up. When you decide what you truly want, release the old stories of "I'm not enough" or "It's too hard," and choose a new story- you invite miracles in and you rewire your mind for success.

A miracle could look like healing a relationship, money showing up when you need it most, or your child suddenly sleeping through the night. It's less about luck and more about alignment.

Becoming a Miracle Maker

You don't have to wait for life to hand you miracles. You get to create them.

Set an intention. Be clear about what you want- not just surviving the week, but thriving.

Feel it now. Imagine the relief, joy, or freedom you'll feel when it happens, and bring that emotion into today.

Trust the process. Even if you don't see instant results, trust that something is shifting beneath the surface.

The Miracle of You

Here's the most important truth: you are a miracle.

Every day, you show up in ways you don't even give yourself credit for. You give, you love, you create space for little humans to grow. That strength, that heart, that persistence- that's miraculous.

So, the next time you wonder if miracles are real, pause. Put your hand on your heart. Look at your child. Look at yourself.

The miracle is already here.

Make SHIFT Happen. Let's GROW.

 ## Mommy Magic Miracle Mantra

"I am the calm in the chaos.
I am the magic in the moment.
My energy is my superpower,
and I create miracles with my presence.
With every breath, I rise, reset, and reconnect
to the powerful mama I was born to be.

A Little Mommy Magic Booster: Therapeutic Hydrogen Water with Frequencies

As a mom, your days are full, your heart is full, and let's be honest- your schedule is overflowing. That's why I love sharing simple tools that support your energy, clarity, and inner calm without adding more to your to-do list. One of those tools is therapeutic molecular hydrogen water infused with gentle, supportive frequencies.

Think of it as a little whisper to your cells: breathe, reset, come back online. Hydrogen is the smallest molecule in the universe, and when you drink hydrogen-rich water, it can support overall cellular balance and help your body handle everyday stress more efficiently. When paired with subtle frequencies, it becomes a beautiful ritual for busy moms something that encourages your system to soften, regulate, and return to flow.

Of course, it's not magic in the fairy-tale sense, but it can feel magical. Moms often describe feeling clearer, lighter, more energized, and more connected to themselves. When your nervous system feels supported, your natural intuition, creativity, and "mom magic" come alive more easily. You respond rather than react. You create rather than cope. You move through the day with a little more grace, a little more glow, and a lot more alignment.

This isn't about perfection. It's about giving your body and mind small moments of nourishment that help you show up as the version of you who feels grounded, vibrant, and capable- because she's always been there. Sometimes she just needs to be activated.

Drink, breathe, reset... and let your magic rise.

More Info @ www.QuantumMemberSHIFT.space

CHAPTER 5

Manipulation – Breaking the Chains of Narcissistic Abuse

Originally this was not going to be part of my book but I felt it was important to add as so many beautiful women and mothers deal with it at one point or another. We tolerate it in our lives and I know first hand it can cause us to dim our light and keep us from fully stepping into our power, purpose and potential.

If you've ever felt like you were losing yourself in a relationship- questioning your memory, doubting your worth, apologizing when you did nothing wrong- you've experienced manipulation. Narcissists thrive on it. Manipulation is their language, their weapon, and their way of staying in control.

What Manipulation Really Is

Manipulation isn't just lying. It's the subtle twisting of reality to make you question your own. It's being told you're "too sensitive" when you point out hurtful behavior. It's being guilted into silence because "you're making things worse." It's promises dangled like carrots- "If you just did this, then I'd be happy with you"- only to keep you chasing approval you'll never get.

It's a game designed so you can't win. And that's the point. The narcissist doesn't want a partner; they want a puppet.

The Common Tactics Narcissists Use

Here are some of the most damaging forms of manipulation you may have faced:

Gaslighting: Making you doubt your memory, sanity, or perception. Example: "I never said that, you must be imagining things."

Guilt-tripping: Making you feel selfish for having needs. Example: "After everything I've done for you, you can't even do this one thing?"

Love-bombing: Over-the-top affection to hook you in, then withdrawing it to keep you desperate for scraps, accepting the bare minimum.

Silent Treatment: Withholding attention or affection to punish you.

Triangulation: Pitting you against others ("Everyone agrees you're the problem") to isolate and control you.

Projection: Accusing you of what they're actually doing. ("You're so manipulative!").

Each tactic has one goal: to break your sense of self so you'll hand over your power.

Why It Works on Good Women

Here's the hard truth: manipulation works because you are loving, empathetic, and hopeful. You see the good in people- you see their potential. You believe in forgiveness and second chances. You want to make the relationship work- for your kids, for your family, for the dream of love you once believed in.

And narcissists exploit that kindness. They don't see your empathy as a gift- they see it as an opening.

But here's the part they never expected: once you see the game, you can never unsee it. And once you stop playing, they lose their power.

Breaking Free from Manipulation

Breaking the cycle doesn't start with changing them- it starts with reclaiming you.

Call It By Its Name: When you recognize manipulation, you stop blaming yourself. Naming it is the first step to freedom.

Detach Emotionally: You can acknowledge their words without absorbing them. Like a storm raging outside- you don't have to go stand in the rain.

Set Boundaries Without Apology: Boundaries aren't about controlling them; they're about protecting you. "No" is a complete sentence.

Rebuild Your Inner Compass: Years of manipulation may have disconnected you from your intuition. Practices like journaling, meditation, and visualization (like the Rapid Recode and Magnetic Mind methods) help you reprogram the beliefs they planted and reconnect to your truth.

Surround Yourself with Reality-Givers: Trusted friends, coaches, or therapists who remind you that you're not crazy, not selfish, not broken- you're healing.

Your Magic Is Stronger

Manipulation is meant to shrink you, but the fact that you're reading this now means it didn't work. You still have your fire. You still have your magic. The narcissist may have tangled you in their web, but webs can be broken and when they are, you rise stronger, wiser, and unstoppable.

Reflection

Take a deep breath, mama.

I want you to pause here and notice how your body feels after reading about manipulation. Do you feel tightness in your chest? A knot in your stomach? Maybe a little shaky? That's your body remembering.

This is important: those sensations are not proof that you're weak. They're proof that you survived. Your nervous system learned to protect you by scanning for danger. You've lived through confusion, blame, and gaslighting, yet here you are- choosing clarity, healing, and freedom.

Recognize that you were never "crazy," "too sensitive," or "selfish." Those were lies planted in you. The real truth? You are resilient. You are intuitive. And your empathy is not a weakness- it's your superpower, once you learn how to protect it.

Journal Prompts

Grab your notebook and write freely or jot it down below - don't worry about spelling or grammar. Let your heart speak.

____

____

____

Where have I noticed manipulation show up in my life? (Gaslighting, guilt-tripping, silent treatment, etc.)

____

____

____

How did I feel in those moments? What story did I begin to believe about myself?

____

____

____

What truth do I want to reclaim instead? (e.g., "I am not selfish, I am allowed to have needs.")

____

____

____

What boundaries do I wish I had in place then? What boundary can I set today?

____

____

____

How does my body feel when I imagine being free from manipulation?

____

____

____

Activation: Reclaiming My Power

This is a short exercise you can do right now to reprogram your mind and body (inspired by the Rapid Recode and Magnetic Mind methods).

Close your eyes. Picture the last time someone tried to manipulate you. Notice the feeling it triggered in your body. Don't run from it-just acknowledge it. Say quietly: "That was manipulation. Not truth."

Imagine cutting the cord. Visualize a cord connecting you to that person's words or actions. Now, with golden scissors in your hand, cut the cord. Watch it fall away. Notice the lightness in your body.

Step into your future self. See yourself one year from now: free, confident, unshakable. What do you look like? How do you carry yourself? What do your kids see when they look at you?

Anchor the feeling. Place your hand on your heart and say:

"I am no longer controlled by manipulation. I see clearly. I stand strong. I am free."

Open your eyes and write down one action you'll take this week to reinforce this freedom- a boundary, a conversation, or simply saying "no" without apology.

✨ Mama, every time you name manipulation, you weaken its grip. Every time you choose yourself, you teach your children what true love looks like. You are breaking cycles. You are creating magic.

Make SHIFT Happen. Let's GROW.

CHAPTER 6

Mirrors & Memories – Releasing the Emotional Charge of Trauma

As mothers, creators, and entrepreneurs of light, we are constantly shaping reality- for our families, our communities, and ourselves. Every thought we hold, every emotion we carry, and every belief we pass down weaves the energetic fabric of the world our children inherit. But to consciously create from love rather than fear, we must first understand the invisible architecture that shapes our experience: **memory and mirrors.**

This chapter invites you to explore how your past is imprinted in your present, and how those imprints- the emotional memories, the trauma, the patterns- become the mirrors reflecting what still asks to be healed. As mompreneurs and manifestors, we're not just building businesses; we're breaking cycles, reprogramming lineage, and embodying new paradigms of power.

Here, you'll learn to see life's reflections not as setbacks, but as sacred teachers - showing you where freedom is waiting to be remembered. Because we cannot create a new future while living from a familiar past. The moment we release the charge of old memories, the mirror shifts- and a new reality, born from awareness, begins to unfold.

Every moment we live carries an echo.

That echo is memory- the energetic imprint of every experience, emotion, and belief we've ever absorbed. These memories don't just live in our minds; they're stored in our cells, our nervous systems, in our DNA and our energetic fields. They shape how we see ourselves, how we respond to life, and what we believe is possible.

For mothers, these memories go even deeper. We not only carry our own emotional history- we often carry generations of untold stories, unresolved pain, and inherited fears. The weight of "what came before us" whispers in our DNA, influencing the choices we make and the limits we unconsciously hold. Epigenomic imprinting even tells us that the thoughts, feelings and emotions of both parents can be imprinted in the DNA weeks before conception. That means for example, if your parents were arguing about money and feeling lots of stress, anxiety and worry, you could potentially be born ready to survive in an environment of lack- born with a scarcity mindset that isn't even yours.

But here's the truth: **memory is not destiny**.

Trauma as Emotional Memory

Trauma is not only what happened to us- it's what remains in us.

It's the emotional charge that never got released, the energy that froze in time when the nervous system said, *"This is too much."*

That emotional charge becomes the lens through which we view life. It colors our reactions, our relationships, our parenting, and even our business decisions. When we carry unresolved trauma, we're not just reacting to the present- we're reliving the past.

This is why we can't create a new future from a familiar past.

If we don't become conscious of the memory patterns running our thoughts, emotions, and actions, we end up recreating the same outcomes- over and over again- just with new faces, new circumstances, and new names. And that is the very definition of insanity- to do the same thing over and over and expect a different result.

The mind clings to what it knows, even when it hurts.

But healing invites us to gently release the charge from those memories so that they no longer define who we are.

The Mirror Effect

Every experience we attract- every challenge, every relationship, every emotional trigger- is a **mirror**.

Life mirrors back to us the beliefs we hold, both consciously and unconsciously. It shows us where love still needs to flow, where forgiveness is waiting to be given, and where the past still controls the present.

When your child pushes your buttons, when a client triggers old insecurity, when money feels scarce- these are not punishments; They're reflections.

They're invitations to pause and ask, *"What memory is this emotion connected to? What story am I still carrying?"*

The mirror doesn't judge. It teaches.

And when we stop resisting what it shows us, healing begins.

Breaking Generational Patterns

As mothers and creators, we have the sacred power to break generational cycles. The trauma that lived through our ancestors does not have to continue through our children. They say it runs in the family; we say this is where it runs out.

When we do the work to heal our emotional memories- through awareness, embodiment, meditation, energy work, and forgiveness- we are not just freeing ourselves; we are reprogramming the lineage.

Our children learn from our energy more than our words. When they see us regulate our emotions, speak our truth, and release the old stories that once defined us, they inherit freedom instead of fear.

Children have mirror neurons. "Monkey see, monkey do." This is why it is so important to teach and lead by example.

Every time we choose love over reaction, presence over projection, compassion over control- we rewrite the energetic script for generations to come.

The Alchemy of Awareness

We can't change that which we aren't aware of but once we are aware we cannot help but change. What we do not change, we are choosing- whether consciously or unconsciously.

Alchemy uses the power of love to transmute a negative energy or experience into a positive one- pain into power and purpose- lessons and experience into knowledge and wisdom so you can move forward.

Healing doesn't mean erasing the past. It means integrating it.

It means looking at the memory with compassion, releasing the emotional charge, and allowing the energy to move through instead of getting trapped.

When we shift from "Why did this happen to me?" to "What is this trying to teach me?" we step out of victimhood and into mastery.

This is the heart of spiritual entrepreneurship- the understanding that your business, your relationships, and your motherhood journey are all mirrors designed to awaken you. Every frustration is feedback. Every obstacle is an opportunity for expansion.

As you release the emotional residue of past memories, your vibration rises. You begin to attract experiences that match your healed state- more peace, more clarity, more abundance.

You become magnetic not because you're striving, but because you're aligned.

From Memory to Mastery

The next time you find yourself stuck in an old loop- repeating patterns, feeling triggered, or doubting your worth- pause.

Breathe.

Ask yourself:

"Is this my present reality... or an old memory replaying itself?"

And then, with love and awareness, choose differently.

Every conscious breath, every act of self-forgiveness, every moment of awareness breaks the spell of the past.

You are not your trauma. You are not your memories. You are not your past.

You are the awareness witnessing them- the consciousness capable of transforming them into wisdom. You are who you choose to become.

When you embrace that truth, life becomes your greatest mirror and your most profound teacher. The past no longer repeats; it reveals.

And from that revelation, your future unfolds- fresh, free, and fully aligned with your soul's purpose.

✦ Key Takeaway:

You cannot create a new future while living from the frequency of your past.

When you release the emotional charge stored in memory, every mirror in your life becomes a portal- from pain to power, from pattern to purpose.

✦ *Mommy Magic Reflection Ritual:*

Releasing Memories, Reclaiming Power

Find a quiet moment- maybe after the kids are asleep, or in that sacred pocket of stillness before the day begins.

Close your eyes.

Take a deep, slow breath in through your nose... and let it out through your mouth.

Feel your body soften.

Feel the energy settle.

Now gently place one hand on your heart and one on your womb- the center of creation and the seat of memory.

Whisper to yourself:

"I am safe to remember.

I am safe to release.

I am safe to rise."

Let any emotion, memory, or tension that surfaces simply *be*. Don't analyze. Don't resist. Just observe- like watching clouds drift across the sky.

If tears come, let them.

If laughter rises, honor it.

You're not reliving the past- you're releasing it.

As you breathe, imagine a soft golden light filling your heart and expanding through your entire body.

This is the light of awareness- the healer within you.

Now say (silently or aloud):

"I honor what I've carried.

I release what no longer serves.

I am the mirror and the light.

I am the memory and the miracle."

Breathe this truth deep into your being.

Visualize your energy field clearing old stories dissolving like mist in sunlight.

When you're ready, open your eyes and place your hands together in gratitude.

Smile softly. You've just rewritten history; not through force, but through love.

✦ **Daily Mantra:**

"I create my future from the frequency of freedom, not the memory of pain."

Mirror Questions for Awareness

Journaling Prompts to Reprogram the Past and Create Your Quantum Future

After you complete the **Mommy Magic Reflection Ritual**, take out your journal and let your thoughts flow freely- no editing, no overthinking. These questions are designed to help you connect the dots between your **memories**, your **mirrors**, and your **manifestations.**

Write from your heart, not your head.

🌙 **1. What emotion keeps repeating in my life right now?**

- Where do I feel this emotion in my body?
- Can I remember the first time I felt it this strongly?

(You're tracing the memory back to its root- awareness begins the release.)

💎 **2. What situations or people trigger me most often?**

- Instead of judging the trigger, ask: *What is this mirroring back to me?*
- What part of me is asking to be seen, loved, or understood?

🌿 **3. What patterns feel inherited - things I've seen in my family line?**

- How might I be carrying emotional energy that isn't fully mine?
- What would it feel like to hand that energy back with love and forgiveness?

🕊️ 4. Where am I still creating from the past?

- What fears, stories, or "truths" about myself keep me stuck in a familiar reality?
- What new story do I choose to tell instead?

🦋 5. What would my future self - healed, free, radiant - want me to know right now?

- What guidance does she whisper when I close my eyes and listen?
- How can I embody that energy *today*?

🕊️ Closing Intention:

Place your hand on your heart and affirm:

"I bless my past with gratitude.
I bless my present with awareness.
I bless my future with infinite possibility.
Every mirror leads me closer to my truth."

These prompts aren't just for writing- they're for awakening.

Each time you revisit them, you'll uncover new layers of healing, release deeper emotional charge, and step closer to your highest potential as a mother, a creator, and a conscious leader. 🌙

You got this. You are loved, you are worthy, you are more than enough and you are far more powerful than you may realize.

Make SHIFT Happen. Let's GROW.

CHAPTER 7

Mindset – Change Your Mind Change Your Reality

Mindset Magic: Rewiring Your Inner World for Success

Being a mompreneur means you're constantly juggling two (or more) full-time jobs, running your business and raising your little ones. You're the CEO, the nurturer, the healer, the strategist, the snack-provider, the conflict mediator and the dreamer. And here's the truth: the difference between burning out and breaking through often comes down to your mindset.

Why Mindset Is Your Magic Wand

Most people try to build their dreams from the outside in, hustling harder, chasing strategies, downloading one more freebie hoping it will be "the one." But here's the problem: if the inner picture in your mind doesn't match the outer results you want, you'll keep hitting invisible walls.

Your subconscious mind holds the real blueprint of your life, beliefs, stories, and identity patterns you've been collecting since you were little. If those beliefs say "I'm not enough," "Success means sacrifice," or "I can't have it all," your efforts will always feel uphill.

Mindset work flips the script. Instead of pushing against those old programs, you rewrite them, aligning your inner world with your truest desires so success becomes natural, not forced.

The Magnetic Mind Shift for Mompreneurs

The Magnetic Mind method (my secret weapon) is built on one core principle: when you align with what you truly desire, without apology, you become magnetic to it.

Here's how you start:

Get radically honest about what YOU want, not what's "practical," not what your family thinks is safe, not what Instagram says is trending.

Create a clear structure for that desire, imagine it vividly, define it, and feel it within you.

Reprogram your subconscious- this is where the Rapid Recode comes in. You identify the old limiting beliefs (the sneaky ones you didn't even realize were running the show) and transform them into empowering truths.

Example: If your belief is "I can't grow my business because I have kids at home," you recode it into "My role as a mom fuels my creativity, focus, and resilience as a business owner."

Mindset Truth for Spiritual Mompreneurs

You don't need to earn your right to thrive. You don't have to sacrifice your peace, your presence with your kids, or your soul's purpose to be successful.

Your business can be a living expression of your truth. Your mindset is the fertile soil where that truth takes root. And when you nurture it, lovingly, intentionally, and consistently, you'll notice that everything starts to shift: your confidence, your opportunities, your income, and your ability to show up as the magical mom and visionary leader you already are.

Mindset Mantra:

"I am worthy of my desires. My dreams are safe with me. I create my life from the inside out."

✨ Mindset Activation: Your 5-Minute Magnetic Reset

This is your quick, anytime-you-need-it ritual to shift from stuck or stressed into aligned and unstoppable.

Step 1- Pause & Breathe

Find a quiet spot (or as quiet as possible in mom-life). Place your hand over your heart. Take three slow, deep breaths, feeling your body relax.

Step 2- Name the Feeling

Say out loud: "Right now, I feel…" and name it- frustrated, anxious, overwhelmed, doubtful. No judgment, just honesty.

Step 3- Spot the Story

Ask yourself: "What am I believing right now that's making me feel this way?" Let the answer come naturally.

Step 4- Recode It

Choose a new truth that feels more empowering. Example: Instead of "I'll never have enough time," shift to "I make powerful progress in the time I have."

Step 5- Step Into It

Close your eyes and imagine your life as if this new truth was already real. Feel the joy, relief, and gratitude as if it's today's reality. The emotional signature of gratitude is "it's already done".

Step 6- Anchor It With Action

Do one small, aligned thing right now that matches your new belief- send the email, post the offer, take the next step.

When you repeat this daily, your nervous system learns that success is safe, joy is normal, and having both a thriving business and a loving family is not only possible- it's inevitable.

💡 **Pro Tip:** The more often you do this, the faster your mind learns to default to your empowered state. You're literally rewiring yourself to be the mompreneur who attracts success with ease.

Living in the Energy of Miracles

Here's a secret most people miss: miracles aren't rare, one-off events. They're not something we have to earn through struggle or hope for in desperate moments. Miracles are simply natural results when your mind, heart, and energy are aligned with your truest desires.

When you shift your mindset, when you choose belief over doubt, vision over fear, you tune into a frequency where opportunities, resources, and connections appear "out of nowhere." But they're not out of nowhere... they've been around you all along. You just couldn't see them through the fog of old beliefs.

Think about it:

That unexpected client who finds you without ads.

The perfect collaboration that "just happens" through a casual conversation.

The breakthrough idea that comes while you're folding laundry or taking a shower.

Those are miracles- the universe rearranging itself to match the version of you who already has what she desires.

The Miracle Mindset in Action

To live in the energy of miracles, you have to:

Expect Them- Wake up each day asking, "I wonder what miracle will show up for me today?"

Release the How- Your job is to hold the vision and take inspired action, not to micromanage the universe.

Celebrate Every Sign- Even the tiniest win is proof you're on the right path. The more you notice and celebrate, the more they multiply.

When you start seeing life through the lens of miracles, motherhood and entrepreneurship stop feeling like an exhausting balancing act. Instead, they become a dance, one where your steps are guided, your load is lighter, and your results feel magical.

Because miracles aren't reserved for "lucky" people. They're for women like you, women who dare to believe they can have it all and are willing to align their inner world until life can't help but reflect it back. Keep shifting your inner world and your unconscious beliefs and your conscious mind and reality will follow. Just remember that the day you plant the seed isn't the day you eat the fruit so keep going and keep GROWING.

✦ Miracle Spotting Journal Prompt

Your mission: For the next 7 days, become a detective for miracles in your life. The more you notice them, the more they'll show up. Practicing gratitude will multiply them. The Matthew Effect, which comes from a verse in the book of Matthew in the Hebrew bible says, "Those who are grateful will be given in abundance and those who are not grateful even what they have will be taken from them". Basically, you don't know what you have until it's gone. Focusing on lack creates more lack. Focusing on the abundance that already surrounds us and expressing an "attitude of gratitude", multiplies our blessings.

Each day, write down:

____

____

____

One miracle you experienced today- big or small.

Examples: An unexpected payment, your child's sudden burst of kindness, the exact solution you needed popping into your mind...

____

____

____

How it made you feel- grateful, excited, relieved, joyful etc...

____

____

____

Why do you think it happened- Was it a result of your new mindset? A coincidence that felt too perfect? Remember though... there is no such thing as a coincidence. Allow the synchronicities to guide you.

____

____

____

What inspired action can you take next to invite more miracles tomorrow?

____

____

____

💡 **Tip**: Keep your journal open throughout the day or use the space below.

Miracles don't always wait until you have a pen in hand.

____

____

____

By the end of the week, you'll see proof that miracles aren't random-they're a natural side effect of living in alignment with your desires. And once you see that clearly, your confidence in creating them will skyrocket.

Make SHIFT Happen. Let's GROW.

Chapter 8

Motivation – You Are the Magic

Motherhood is often described as a miracle but many moms forget that they themselves are the miracle. Between diaper changes, sleepless nights, endless laundry, and the quiet sacrifices no one sees, it's easy to lose touch with that inner spark. But here's the truth: the magic you're searching for has always been inside you. Here are some of my favorite quotes to remind us of our power and motivate us to stay focused.

Napoleon Hill, author of Think and Grow Rich, reminds us that, "Whatever the mind can conceive and believe it can achieve.".

The Power of Imagination

Neville Goddard taught that imagination is not child's play- it's creation itself. He said, "Imagination creates reality." Every time you picture your children thriving, every time you imagine yourself calm and radiant instead of stressed and overwhelmed, you are shaping the reality you step into. Remember- "Feeling is the Secret."

**"Imagination is the beginning of creation.
You imagine what you desire, you will what you imagine and at last you create what you will."
—George Bernard Shaw**

Albert Einstein, one of the greatest minds of all time, understood the creative force within us. He said, "Imagination is more important than knowledge. For knowledge is limited, whereas imagination encircles the world. Imagination is everything. It is a preview of life's coming attractions".

For mothers, this is a powerful reminder: you don't need to have all the answers, the perfect parenting manual, or the flawless routine. What matters is the vision you hold for your children and yourself.

Einstein also taught, "The most important decision we make is whether we believe we live in a friendly or hostile universe." When you choose to see life as supportive, not against you, the universe begins to reflect that belief back. And perhaps his most reassuring reminder is this: "A person who never made a mistake never tried anything new." Motherhood is filled with mistakes, but each one is proof that you're growing, learning, and creating a life of love.

Leonardo da Vinci, a master of both art and science, once said, "Where the spirit does not work with the hand, there is no art." Motherhood is an art form and when your spirit (your imagination, your inner world) aligns with your actions, everything you touch becomes infused with love and brilliance. He also said that we aren't crazy, we are awake in a crazy world.

The Subconscious Secret

Dr. Joseph Murphy explained, "The subconscious mind cannot take a joke. It takes you at your word." This means that every time you say, "I'm exhausted," "I can't do this," or "I'm not enough," your subconscious hears it as truth. But you can rewire this. By choosing new, empowering thoughts- "I am strong," "I am supported," "I am love"- you reprogram your inner world, which changes the outer. He said, "ignorance is the only sin and suffering is the consequence". It's time to turn our ignorance into power.

Carl Jung echoed this when he said, "Until you make the unconscious conscious, it will rule your life and you will call it fate." The Rapid Recode process teaches exactly this by uncovering the old patterns running your life and rewriting them into something beautiful.

The Wisdom of the Ancients

Aristotle believed, "We are what we repeatedly do. Excellence, then, is not an act, but a habit." Mommy magic doesn't come from one big moment of breakthrough, it comes from the daily practice of choosing joy, peace, and presence.

Socrates said, "The unexamined life is not worth living." For mothers, this means pausing long enough to notice- what stories am I telling myself? Am I living in survival, or am I creating from desire? He also said, "The secret to change isn't to focus our energy on fighting the old, but on creating the new."

Where Focus Goes, Energy Flows. What We Focus On EXPANDS.

Buddha taught, "What we imagine, we create. What we feel, we attract. What we think, we become." And Jesus reminded us, "According to your faith, be it unto you." And "As a man thinketh so shall he become." Both point to the same truth: your beliefs shape your world.

The Shift Into Magic

Wayne Dyer often reminded us, "Change the way you look at things, and the things you look at change." A sink full of dishes can be evidence of overwhelm, or it can be a sign of abundance- that your family is fed, that your children are alive and thriving. The shift is inside you, and it ripples out into everything around you. We can reframe our world because we don't actually see the world as it is; we see it as we are.

Nikola Tesla, the genius inventor and visionary, revealed the hidden truth behind creation when he said, "If you want to find the secrets of the universe, think in terms of energy, frequency and vibration." This wisdom applies directly to motherhood: the energy you carry in your body, the vibration of your thoughts, and the frequency of your emotions ripple through your home and into your children. Tesla also reminded us, "The day science begins to study non-physical phenomena, it will make more progress in one decade than in all the previous centuries of its existence." In many ways, this is the essence of mommy magic- understanding that the unseen world of belief, love, and energy shapes your family's reality more than anything else.

When you begin to live from your true desires- not just obligation or survival- you step into alignment with who you really are. And that's when the magic happens.

As Dr. Joe Dispenza reminds us, "Your personality creates your personal reality." When you change the thoughts you think, the feelings you hold, and the energy you carry, you transform the life you experience. "We cannot create a new future stuck in a familiar past." "Our mind can either be a record of the past or a MAP to the future." Let's not be creatures of habit, but creators of habits. (Be sure to visit my website to get your FREE M.A.P.- Miracle Action Plan) www.QuantumMemberSHIFT.space

✨ **Practice for Mommy Magic:** Tonight, before bed, close your eyes. Imagine your ideal day as a mother- not the perfect house, but the perfect feeling. Maybe it's laughter at breakfast, a moment of peace during naptime, or your child running into your arms. Feel it fully. Breathe it in. Let your subconscious take this as truth. You are rewiring your reality with every thought and feeling.

Make SHIFT Happen. Let's GROW.

CHAPTER 9

Money & Monetization – Millionaire Mindset

Money. For so many mompreneurs, it's the thing that feels both exciting and scary at the same time. We want it, we dream about it, but we also wrestle with guilt, old beliefs, and that nagging voice that whispers: Who am I to charge for this or to get paid in easy, fun ways by me just being who I am, sharing what I love and helping others grow?

Let's be real- money is not just numbers in a bank account. It's safety. It's security. It's energy. It's flow. It's an amplifier of who you already are. And as a spiritual mompreneur, money isn't something you "take" from others- it's something you circulate. It flows through you as an exchange of value, gratitude, and impact.

The Old Stories About Money

Many of us grew up with limiting money stories:

"Money doesn't grow on trees."

"Rich people are greedy."

"You have to work hard and sacrifice to make money."

"Money is the root of all evil."

These old beliefs don't just live in your head- they live in your subconscious. And unless you rewrite them, they'll quietly sabotage your business, no matter how hard you work.

Here's the truth: Money is not good or bad. It simply magnifies the heart of the person who holds it. If you're generous, aligned, and heart-led, more money in your hands means more generosity, alignment, and impact in the world.

Monetization as Sacred Exchange

To monetize your gifts is to honor them. When someone invests in your coaching, your program, or your product, they're not just paying for a service. They are declaring: I am ready. I am committed. I believe in myself.

That exchange is sacred. When you undercharge or give away your magic for free, you actually rob people of the transformation they're seeking- because they never fully invest.

Your role as a spiritual mompreneur is to create containers (offers, programs, services) where transformation can happen, and to price them in alignment with the value they deliver.

The Magnetic Money Mindset

This is where your inner work comes in. Using principles from the Magnetic Mind method:

Alignment with True Desires – Stop creating offers from fear ("What will sell?") and start creating from alignment ("What do I desire to bring into the world?").

Recode Your Subconscious – When old beliefs like "I can't charge that much" come up, use recoding practices to shift them into empowering truths: "I create abundance for my family and my clients."

Emotional Mastery – Money triggers a lot of emotions like fear, guilt, scarcity, worry, frustration etc. Learn to sit with them, master them, and shift back into the energy of abundance.

Take Aligned Action – Set your prices, share your offers, and invite people in with confidence. Clarity creates clients.

Practical Steps to Monetization

The Millionaire Mindset:

Having a millionaire mindset isn't about obsessing over dollars, it's about expanding your identity. A millionaire doesn't just think, "How do I make money?" She thinks, "How do I create impact and systems that allow abundance to multiply?" She plays the long game, sees opportunities where others see obstacles, and never apologizes for wanting more. The millionaire mindset is about stepping into the version of you who already has financial freedom, making decisions from that place of confidence, vision, and abundance rather than fear or scarcity. When you begin to embody that energy, money starts to respond differently. You stop chasing it, and instead, you magnetize it.

Habits of the Millionaire Mompreneur 

Thinks in Expansion, Not Limitation:

Instead of asking, "Can I afford this?" she asks, "How can I create the resources for this?"

Invests in Herself First:

She knows her business grows at the speed of her mindset. Books, coaching, programs- she invests because she understands she is her greatest asset.

Values Time Over Money:

A millionaire mom doesn't try to do everything herself. She outsources what drains her so she can focus on her zone of genius and family.

Acts as If:

She makes decisions from the identity of her future self- the woman who already has abundance, not the one who's still hustling to get there.

Celebrates Money:

Every dollar, whether $5 or $5,000, is celebrated with gratitude. This keeps her energy magnetic and her flow of money open.

Focuses on Impact First, Money Second:

She understands that money is the natural byproduct of solving problems, serving deeply, and creating real transformation. Work for love not money and the money will come. Follow your passion to find your purpose and your purpose will provide you provision.

Stays Emotionally Resilient:

Challenges happen, launches flop, clients/customers ghost, but instead of spiraling, she recalibrates quickly. Her worth is never tied to temporary outcomes.

Keeps Money in Circulation:

She gives, saves, invests, and spends in alignment. She knows money is like breath- you inhale and exhale. Holding too tightly chokes the flow.

Here's how to begin monetizing your magic:

Money Magic Monetization in Action

This is designed to help you rewrite old money stories, align your offers, and magnetize abundance into your business. Grab a journal and answer these prompts honestly- no sugarcoating.

Rewrite Your Money Story

What did I learn about money growing up? (List at least 3 beliefs you heard at home, school, or church.)

____

____

____

Which of these beliefs still show up in my business today?

____

____

____

What new empowering money beliefs do I choose instead?

✨ Example: "Money is hard to earn" → "Money flows easily when I create from alignment."

____

____

____

Choose Your Core Offer – Don't overwhelm yourself with ten different products. Start with one transformational offer you can stand behind 100%. I can help you with this if you decide to join one of my teams or you may already have product and services to offer.

Price with Alignment – Instead of asking, "What will people pay?" ask, "What feels expansive for me and empowering for them?"

Create Multiple Pathways – Some clients want a taste (like a workshop), some want a meal (a group program), and some want the whole feast (private coaching). Offer different levels of access to your magic. Multiple pathways- multiple sources of income.

Let Money Flow – Make it easy for people to pay you. Set up simple systems (PayPal, Stripe, etc.) and celebrate every transaction as a sign of energy flowing.

The Mommy Magic of Wealth

As moms, we sometimes feel guilt around making money, like we're taking time or energy away from our family. But here's the reframe: every dollar you earn through your soul-aligned business is a gift to your family. It's proof to your children that it's possible to live with purpose and prosperity.

When your kids see you building a business from love, integrity, and alignment, they learn the most powerful money lesson of all: that abundance and impact are not separate. They're connected.

Money is not the end goal- it's the fuel. It gives you the freedom to say "yes" to your desires, to invest in your dreams, and to create the life you truly want. And that, mama, is the real magic.

✨ Affirmation for the Aligned Mompreneur:

"I honor my gifts by charging for them. Money flows to me with ease because I create impact, transformation, and love in the world."

List 3 ways people can currently access your magic:

1. A taste (free or low-ticket offer, like a workshop, mini-course, or eBook).

____

____

____

2. A meal (your main offer: group coaching, program, or service).

____

____

____

3. A feast (high-touch: private coaching, mastermind, or VIP day).
   ➞ Which of these do I want to focus on growing first?

____

____

____

4. **Magnetize Your First $5K (or Next $5K)**

   My income goal for the next 30 days is: $_______

   My core offer is: ________________

   Price of my offer: $_______

   To reach my goal, I need _____ clients.

Daily aligned actions I commit to:
(Keep this simple—3 consistent actions done daily are more powerful than 30 inconsistent ones!)

____

____

____

5. **Celebration Practice** 🎉

Money is energy. The more you celebrate it, the more it flows.

Write 3 ways you will celebrate every time money comes in (no matter how small). Example: light a candle, dance to a song, write "thank you" in your journal.

____

____

____

✦ Bonus Affirmation:

"I am worthy of receiving money for my magic. Every dollar that flows to me creates more love, impact, and abundance in the world. I make money while I sleep. Abundance is my birthright.- Thank You Thank You Thank You."

Now let's get into Magnetic Marketing.

Make SHIFT Happen. Let's GROW.

CHAPTER 10

Magnetic Marketing – Brand Yourself & Attract Your Soul Tribe

Attracting Your Dream Clients & Customers With Ease

As a spiritual mompreneur, you already know that business is more than transactions- it's transformation. The same way your heart pulls you toward your true desires, your business can magnetically pull the right clients toward you. This isn't about chasing leads or hustling until you're burnt out; it's about becoming so aligned, so authentically YOU, that the perfect people can't help but be drawn into your world.

The Heart of Magnetic Marketing

Magnetic marketing is the soulful sister to the Magnetic Mind method- it's marketing that works from the inside out.

Instead of asking, "How can I convince people to buy from me?", you ask, "How can I show up so aligned with my message that my people instantly feel they've found 'their' coach, guide, or service provider?"

Here's the magic: when you align your business with your true desires (not what you think you should be doing), you create an energetic signal that your dream clients pick up on- even if they've never met you before. They feel you. They trust you. They want what you offer because it resonates with their soul.

The **80/20 principle** is pure mommy magic when it comes to money and marketing. It reminds you that you don't need to do *everything-*

you just need to do the right things. Eighty percent of your results often come from just twenty percent of your effort. That means more flow, less hustle. More intention, less overwhelm. When you focus on the few aligned actions that actually move the needle- sharing your message authentically, showing up where your people are, and creating offers that feel good- you naturally attract more abundance without burning yourself out. The magic isn't in doing more; it's in choosing wisely, staying aligned, and letting your energy do the heavy lifting. Do less and accomplish more by taking only the most powerful, aligned, intentional, inspired actions. Consistency is key.

The 5 Pillars of Magnetic Marketing for Mompreneurs

1. Alignment with Your True Desire

Just like in the Magnetic Mind process, it starts with getting crystal clear on what you actually want- not just for your business, but for your lifestyle, your family, and your soul.

If your heart longs for spacious mornings with your kids, high-value clients who respect your time, and the freedom to take Friday off, your marketing should reflect that energy. This clarity becomes your brand's backbone.

Pro Tip: Write down your dream day in vivid detail. Then, build your offers and messaging around making that dream day your normal.

2. Your Creative Structure

In marketing, your creative structure is the framework that communicates your value clearly and consistently. Think of it as your brand's home- warm, welcoming, and uniquely yours.

You need:

A clear core message – One that speaks directly to your ideal client's heart and soul.

A signature offer – The transformation you guide clients through, packaged in a way that feels irresistible.

A storytelling rhythm – Consistent posts, emails, or videos that share your journey, client wins, and authentic insights.

3. Reprogramming Marketing Mindset Blocks

Most mompreneurs secretly carry limiting beliefs about marketing: I'm not a natural salesperson, I'm too busy with the kids to be consistent, or nobody will pay me high-ticket prices.

These thoughts are just mental programming, and they can be recoded.

Magnetic marketing requires you to see marketing not as a chore, but as an act of love. Every post, every email, every offer is an invitation for someone to change their life. The moment you release the belief that marketing is "pushy," you unlock your ability to sell with soul-heart centered entrepreneurship.

4. Emotional Energy in Your Messaging

Clients don't buy your product, they buy the feeling they believe it will give them. People don't want INFORMATION; They want TRANSFORMATION.

Whether it's peace of mind, confidence, freedom, or joy, you need to infuse your marketing with the emotional payoff. When you post on social media, don't just describe your offer, describe the life it helps them create.

Example: Instead of "I offer 1:1 coaching sessions," say, "Imagine waking up without that knot of stress in your chest, knowing exactly how to create the life you've been dreaming of. That's what we'll build together."

5. Action + Accountability

Magnetic marketing isn't about doing everything- it's about doing the right things consistently.

Pick 1–2 main platforms where your dream clients hang out, show up with intention, and track what works. Create small, doable action steps each week and hold yourself accountable, just like you would with a client.

Why Magnetic Marketing Works for Moms

When you market from alignment rather than desperation, you create a business that supports your life and not the other way around.

Your energy becomes your best marketing tool. When you're lit up about what you do, people feel it. When you post with joy instead of obligation, people notice. And when you believe deeply in the transformation you offer, people trust you. Be the energy you want to attract.

A Soulful Challenge for You

This week, try this:

Write down your true desire for your business and life.

____

____

____

Post one piece of content that shares your heart, your story, and why you do what you do.

____

____

____

Notice who leans in, comments, or reaches out. That's your magnet working.

____

____

____

Remember: Your dream clients are already looking for you. Your only job is to make it easy for them to find you.

❇ Magnetic Marketing Mantra for Mompreneurs

(Read this every morning before you open your laptop or post online.)

I am magnetic to my dream clients.
My energy radiates confidence, clarity, and love.
I show up authentically, and the right people feel my presence.
My offers are valuable, transformative, and aligned with my purpose.
Every word I share carries the vibration of transformation.
I trust the flow of clients, opportunities, and abundance into my life.
Marketing is not a chore, it is an act of service.
I attract with ease. I serve with joy. I receive with gratitude.

❇ Soul-Aligned Social Post Formula

Step 1 – Open with the Heart (Connection)

Begin with a short, emotional hook that makes your audience feel seen.

Examples:

"If you've ever felt like you're running a business while running on fumes, this is for you."

"To the mom who's been praying for a sign... here it is."

"I see you, trying to grow your dream without missing bedtime stories."

Step 2 – Share Your Story (Authenticity)

In 3–5 sentences, share a personal struggle or turning point that relates to your offer.

Example:

"I used to think marketing meant forcing myself to post daily, even when I felt exhausted. Then I discovered a way to share from the heart, and clients started finding me without the hustle."

Step 3 – Show the Transformation (Inspiration)

Paint a vivid before-and-after picture so they can feel the result.

Example:

"Now, I attract clients who respect my time, pay my worth, and align with my energy. I get to work from home, make a difference, and still be present with my kids."

Step 4 – Invite Them Closer (Action)

Offer them a next step that feels like a gift, not a pitch.

Examples:

"If this speaks to you, comment 'MAGNETIC' and I'll send you a free mini-training."

"DM me the word 'READY' and let's chat about what your magnetic marketing plan could look like."

"I'm opening 3 spots for private coaching this month- message me to see if one's yours."

Pro Tip: Always pair your post with a photo of you-smiling, working, or with your kids. People buy from people they can see and connect with.

Post 1 – From Hustle to Flow

Connection:

If you've ever felt like you're running a business while running on fumes, this is for you.

Authenticity:

I used to believe that success meant posting every single day, saying yes to every client, and working late into the night while my kids slept. I thought hustle was the only way to grow.

Transformation:

When I shifted into marketing from alignment- sharing my story, speaking to my dream clients, and letting my energy do the attracting, everything shifted. Now, my business runs with flow instead of force. I get to create my own schedule and spend time doing what I love with the people I love the most.

Action:

If you're ready to stop chasing clients and start attracting them, comment MAGNETIC below and I'll share a free mini-training that shows you how.

Post 2 – The Mom Who Almost Quit

Connection:

To the mom who's one late bill away from giving up on her business dream… I see you.

Authenticity:

A year ago, I sat at my kitchen table with my head in my hands, wondering if I should just call it quits. I was exhausted, underpaid, and what felt like invisible online.

Transformation:

Then I learned how to market in a way that felt like me. I started telling my story, sharing my heart, and unapologetically inviting people into my world. Within months, I made my first 6 figures and the freedom to actually enjoy my business.

Action:

If this resonates, DM me the word READY and I'll tell you the exact first step I took to turn it all around.

Post 3 – Your Clients Are Looking for You

Connection:

You don't have to shout to be heard- you just have to shine.

Authenticity:

I used to feel invisible online. I was posting because I "had to," not because I had something to say. And guess what? People scrolled right past me.

Transformation:

When I started marketing with soul, sharing my truth, focusing on my dream clients, and letting go of the pressure to please everyone- everything shifted. People began reaching out, saying, "I feel like you're speaking directly to me."

Action:

If you want your dream clients to feel that way about you, comment SHINE and I'll send you my 3 favorite magnetic post ideas to get started.

✷ 7-Day Magnetic Marketing Content Map

Day 1 – Heart Hook Story

Purpose: Build emotional connection and let people see the real you.

Example Prompt: Share a personal moment that shaped your business journey (struggle → shift → success).

Caption Starter: "If you've ever felt [insert relatable struggle], you're not alone..."

Day 2 – Client Transformation Spotlight

Purpose: Show proof of results & inspire belief.

Example Prompt: Share a short success story from a client or even from your own transformation.

Caption Starter: "When [client's name or 'a mom I worked with'] first came to me, she felt..."

Day 3 – Myth Busting Post

Purpose: Position yourself as a trusted expert by challenging a common belief.

Example Prompt: Share a myth about your industry and replace it with a truth that supports your audience.

Caption Starter: "You don't need [insert common myth] to [insert desired outcome]..."

Day 4 – Behind-the-Scenes Peek

Purpose: Humanize your brand & show the real life of a mompreneur.

Example Prompt: Share a candid photo of your workspace, your kids in the background, or your morning coffee ritual.

Caption Starter: "This is what running my business looks like today..."

Day 5 – Value Nugget / Quick Tip

Purpose: Give quick, actionable value to your audience.

Example Prompt: Share one simple tip they can use right away to get closer to their goal.

Caption Starter: "Here's one thing you can do today to [insert result]..."

Day 6 – Invitation to Work With You

Purpose: Clearly ask for the sale in a heart-centered way.

Example Prompt: Share the transformation your offer provides and invite them to take the next step.

Caption Starter: "Imagine if in 3 months you could [insert dream result]..."

Day 7 – Magnetic Mindset Share

Purpose: Infuse your audience with belief & positive energy.

Example Prompt: Share your Magnetic Marketing Mantra or a personal affirmation that inspires you.

Caption Starter: "Here's what I remind myself every single morning..."

💡 Pro Tip for Readers:

Post at least 1 personal photo of yourself each week.

End every post with a call-to-action (comment, DM, click link).

Reuse content from previous weeks- your dream clients often need to hear your message multiple times before they act.

You may also want to consider using a platform like systeme.io for email marketing, a CRM and automation in your business to free up time, nurture your leads and ultimately create more sales on autopilot.

Stop chasing and forcing and become an attraction magnet for your dream, soul aligned clients. Personally I like to refer to them as my friends- my soul tribe. Contracts have been set in place for them to arrive in divine perfect timing. Call them in. They are waiting for you.

Attraction Marketing Mantra

I desire to attract thee most badass spiritually alive souls into my businesses to create real and lasting change in our lives and aspire to inspire others to do the same."

Make SHIFT Happen. Let's GROW.

CHAPTER 11

Mastery and Momentum – Keep Going Keep GROWING: The Power of Consistency

The Twin Engines of Your Mompreneur Journey

Motherhood teaches us a secret most people never discover: momentum doesn't come from waiting until you "feel ready." Momentum is born in the tiny, messy, everyday steps you take when the kids are screaming, the laundry's piled high, and your dream business still feels like a whisper in your heart.

As a spiritual mompreneur, you're not just building a business-you're crafting a legacy of freedom, impact, and alignment. To do this, you need two powerful forces working in your favor: momentum and mastery.

Momentum: The Magic of Imperfect Action

Momentum is energy in motion. It's the decision to post your offer, even if your hair's a mess. It's hitting "publish" on your new website, even though it's not perfect. It's choosing to show up live for your audience with love, instead of waiting for everything to align.

Here's the truth: momentum doesn't come from perfection. It comes from permission, the permission you give yourself to move forward, no matter how small the step feels.

Think of momentum as a snowball rolling down a hill. At first, it's tiny, fragile, and easy to stop. But with each action, each conversation, each email, each video, the snowball gathers speed, size, and unstoppable power. That's the energy that carries you when motivation fades.

Spiritual Reframe: Momentum is you telling the Universe, "I trust myself. I trust my dream. I'm moving, and I know support will meet me along the way."

Mastery: The Art of Becoming

Mastery isn't about never making mistakes. It's about deepening your relationship with your craft, your business, and yourself.

True mastery for a mompreneur means:

Emotional Mastery: learning to redirect self-doubt, fear, or guilt into energy that fuels your vision. (Remember, your emotions are powerful creative fuel. When mastered, they magnetize your desires faster.)

Subconscious Mastery: rewiring the old stories- "I'm not good enough," "I can't have success and be a great mom," or "I don't have time." Through tools like the Rapid Recode, you release those old identities and step into the woman who already has what she wants.

Creative Mastery: living from your "true choice" instead of circumstance. This means building your business from your heart's desire, not from pressure, comparison, or what others say you "should" do.

Mastery is not a finish line. It's a way of being. Each day you show up, you are becoming the master of your own creation.

The Dance of Momentum and Mastery

Momentum without mastery can feel frantic- like running on a hamster wheel.

Mastery without momentum can feel stagnant- like waiting for life to give you permission.

But together? They create a beautiful rhythm.

Momentum gives you movement.

Mastery gives you direction.

One without the other keeps you stuck. Together, they make you magnetic.

Mommy Magic Practice: Align and Activate

Here's a simple daily ritual to weave momentum and mastery into your day:

Set Your True Choice: Each morning, choose who you want to BE today as a mompreneur (e.g., "I am a confident, inspiring leader.").

Recode the Old Story: Notice any resistance or limiting belief that comes up. Pause. Take a breath. Say, "That's the old me. I now choose to create from my true desire."

Take One Imperfect Action: Post the thing, message the client, record the video. Action births momentum.

Celebrate the Micro-Win: Before bed, acknowledge the progress you made, no matter how small. This builds self-trust and anchors mastery.

Remember that the day we plant the seed isn't the day we eat the fruit. Rome wasn't built in a day. Creation takes time but cultivate those seeds in the garden of your mind and they will come to fruition- we always reap what we sow. There is a process to creation- we live in a 3D world where it takes time to move through space- it takes time to move from one point of consciousness to another. But here is the perfect example of momentum...

Chinese bamboo grows underground for five years. If you do not take care of it meticulously it will die underground and never come to fruition. Be consistent with its care and after those five years, it finally breaks through the ground and shoots up over 90 feet within the first few weeks. THAT'S the power of momentum- The COMPOUND effect.

Mastery and Momentum in Alignment =
Quantum Leaps in Your Life and Business.

Final Word

As a spiritual mompreneur, your journey is not about hustling harder. It's about aligning deeper. Momentum will carry you forward when you feel tired. Mastery will remind you that you're not just building a business- you're becoming the woman your children will look up to as proof that dreams are worth pursuing.

Remember, mama: momentum starts with your next brave step. Mastery unfolds in every step that follows. Together, they'll carry you into the abundant, magnetic life you were born to create.

And if someone hasn't told you today: I love you and you are more than worthy. Straighten your crown and...

"Keep on truckin. Life is a highway and we're gonna ride it all night long."

(Quoted in Loving Memory of Randy Reichert)

This is only the beginning.

The journey of a thousand miles starts with the first step.

Make SHIFT Happen. Let's GROW.

CHAPTER 12

Movement – Join the EVOLution rEVOLution

Your Next Step Into Mommy Magic

Mama, you've poured yourself into everyone else for so long. You've been the cook, the chauffeur, the comforter, the teacher, the nurse, the referee, the conflict mediator and the never-ending giver. But now, you've begun to remember something powerful: you are more than just a mom. You are a woman with dreams, desires, and magic waiting to be unleashed.

This journey we've taken together isn't about adding more to your already full plate. It's about reshaping the way you see yourself, reclaiming your energy, and stepping back into your power. Because when YOU rise, everything around you rises too- your kids, your relationships, your happiness.

But here's the truth: transformation doesn't happen overnight, and it doesn't happen alone. The old patterns, the self-doubt, the guilt- they don't disappear just because you read a book or do one exercise. They fade when you stay supported, guided, and held accountable.

That's why your next step is everything.

✨ If you're craving gentle, steady progress with ongoing support, join me for Weekly Coaching & Accountability where you'll get the encouragement and structure you need to keep moving forward without losing yourself along the way.

✨ Or, if you're ready to go ALL IN and create a completely new reality in record time, step into the Total Shift Experience where you'll rewrite the patterns that have kept you stuck and design the life you've secretly been wishing for.

Both paths lead to the same destination: a life where YOU feel alive, empowered, and magnetic, without sacrificing the love and presence you give your family.

And here's the beautiful part, this isn't just about you. It's about all of us. Every time a mother returns to herself, she sparks a ripple effect of healing, wholeness, and love. Together, we're creating a movement- a return to self, a love revolution, an EVOLution rEVOLution- where women rise not in spite of being mothers, but because of the power it awakens in them. This is bigger than one woman's transformation. It's a collective uprising of love, strength, and unapologetic self-worth.

We are breaking generational curses and patterns- trading in our generational trauma for generational wealth.

So, mama, take this as your invitation. Don't let the momentum stop here. You've already opened the door- now it's time to walk through it.

Your magic is real. Your desires are worthy. And the world needs the most radiant version of you.

☞ Choose your next step today- Weekly Coaching & Accountability or 90 Days to Transformation The Shift Method and let's make this YOUR season of unstoppable growth.

Because you're not just raising babies. You're raising yourself into the woman you were always meant to be.

Make SHIFT Happen. Let's GROW.

About the Author

I'm Andrea 😃 the Magnetic Mompreneur 🧲

Quantum Manifestation Coach Spiritual Mindset Mentor & Holistic Wellness Advocate
I am a 39 year old homebirthing unschooling momprenuer of 4 from Pennsylvania
I am an International and Amazon best selling author Dream Big Do Bigger Build the Bridge Between YourDreams and Reality 🦄🧲 and my upcoming book Dumbed Down Drugged Up and Disempowered Awakening & Making the Shift into the New 5D Earth Paradigm being released June 2025
I share content on mindset, spirituality, personal development, entrepreneurship, homebirth, unschooling, consciousness, online business & more ⚛️
I am completely obsessed with human transformation and the process of creation and I AM on a mission to SHIFT the consciousness of humanity 🐛🦋

If you're on a holistic health and wellness, spiritual awakening journey...
YOU'RE IN THE RIGHT PLACE

There is a REVOLUTION upon us and you may be hearing the call to fulfill a higher purpose, be of service and create CHANGE in the world I got the call many years ago and have been following my passion and living my purpose ever since

Now I am here to help guide others
I am a superconscious creator & transformation accelerator. I help you awaken to your divine soul truth, find your purpose & take your

power back. I help momprenuers & spiritual entrepreneurs specifically, to overcome limited programming & make their dreams reality

Making Dreams Reality

I can help you ditch toxins from your home, mind, body and spirit AFFORDABLY to heal, transform, and create a life that you love
This video is a little about me, what I do and how I can potentially assist you on your journey to
Total Wellness & Transformation
Making the Shift Magick Miracles & Alchemy Quantum Manifestation Coaching
Spiritual Mindset & Holistic Wellness

In January 2020 I made the decision to become a coach and since then I've studied all things mindset and spirituality and I've become a Transformational Master Quantum Manifestation Coach Spiritual Mindset Mentor Intuitive Healer & Akashic Records Practitioner certified in Nuerolinguistic Programming Emotional Freedom Tapping & Time Techniques Life & Success Coaching as well as Hypnotherapy & the Magnetic Mind Method. I'm also currently attending Maharishi International University for my bachelor's in consciousness and human potential

As a Certified Magnetic Mind Coach, I use the five steps to conscious creation superconscious transformation recode method to rewire the brain and recode your DNA. It is based on proven neuroscience, epigenetics, and quantum physics along side spiritual concepts of universal law and alchemy to help you release limiting beliefs, toxic emotions and resistance. This allows you to become an attraction magnet and move towards your desired reality in complete ease, grace, and flow
I'm also the Fearless Humble leader of Miracle Mavens helping moms create time & financial freedom. My personal mission is to transform the world one person at a time starting with myself

We are being dumbed down drugged up & disempowered & I am committed to helping people awaken to their full potential & raising the vibration of the planet to shift us into the new 5D paradigm "heaven on earth"

Disclaimer

I always encourage everyone to do their own research and form their own beliefs. Your beliefs are POWERFUL they create your reality. Take what resonates and leave the rest. If your beliefs are serving you well, if you are creating and living a life that you love or moving towards it, more power to you If not you've got to take a look at your mindset.

☞ You've done the inner work. Now it's time to turn your *healing* into *impact*.

Step into your power with *Mommy Magic* – step into the space that helps spiritual moms align their mindset, energy, and purpose so they can create the life and business they're meant for.

✨ Your magic isn't just for you... it's meant to be shared with the world.

You were never meant to fit into the system - you were meant to *shift it*.

🗣 Join the movement at
www.QuantumMemberSHIFT.space

www.ingramcontent.com/pod-product-compliance
Lightning Source LLC
Chambersburg PA
CBHW071331030726
47594CB00002B/632